KU-166-106

CALM
and
MINDFULNESS

A Helen Exley
QUOTATION COLLECTION

Helen Exley

ILLUSTRATED BY JULIETTE CLARKE
EDITED BY HELEN EXLEY
THE MINDFULNESS EXERCISES ARE ALL WRITTEN BY
DALTON EXLEY ©HELEN EXLEY CREATIVE LTD 2017.
Published in 2017 by Helen Exley®LONDON in Great Britain.
Illustrated by Juliette Clarke ©Helen Exley Creative Ltd 2017
Design and creation by Helen Exley ©Helen Exley Creative
Ltd 2017. All the words by Pam Brown, Dalton Exley, Charlotte
Gray, Harold Dalton, Helen Exley, Helen Thomson, Helen M. Exley
and D. E. Harold are © Helen Exley Creative Ltd 2017.

ISBN 978-1-78485-143-9

12 11 10 9 8 7 6 5 4 3 2 1

The moral right of the author has been asserted.
A copy of the CIP data is available from the British Library on request.
All rights reserved. No part of this publication may be reproduced
or transmitted in any form or by any means, electronic or mechanical,
including photocopy, recording or any information storage and
retrieval system without permission in writing from the Publisher.
Printed in China.

OTHER BOOK IN THE SERIES
LIVE! LOVE! LAUGH!   RESILIENCE   POSITIVE THOUGHTS
BELIEVE in YOURSELF   FOREVER TOGETHER

Helen Exley®LONDON, 16 Chalk Hill,
Watford, Hertfordshire, WD19 4BG, UK.
www.helenexley.com

Mindfulness is about love
and loving life.
When you cultivate this love,
it gives you clarity
and compassion for life.

JON KABAT-ZINN, B. 1944

Love the moment.
Flowers grow out of dark moments.
Therefore, each moment is vital.
It affects the whole.
Life is a succession
of such moments and to live each,
is to succeed.

CORITA KENT 1918 - 1986

THE MINDFULNESS EXERCISE

Be aware of your breath, of breathing:
there's nothing "to do". Be mindful of
your breathing, that's all.
Sit with both feet on the ground,
your hands on your lap.
Bring all your attention to breathing.
Notice the air entering your nose,
going to your lungs and leaving again.
This exercise isn't about relaxation,
but this is often a welcome side-effect.
Become an observer of yourself.
Do this for a few minutes each day,
don't time it, just do this till you've
had enough of it – even noting thoughts
as they pop into your head.

DALTON EXLEY

Mindfulness is the aware, balanced acceptance of the present experience. It isn't more complicated than that. It is opening to or receiving the present moment, pleasant or unpleasant, just as it is, without either clinging to it or rejecting it.

SYLVIA BOORSTEIN

Sit
Rest
Work.

Alone with yourself,
Never weary.

On the edge of the forest
Live joyfully,
Without desire.

GAUTAMA BUDDHA c.563 B.C. – 483 B.C.

There is great happiness in not wanting, in not being something, in not going somewhere.

JIDDU KRISHNAMURTI 1895 – 1986

Sometimes I listen to the silence, gaze at the light falling on a plaster wall, a patch of woody grass or the clouds moving across a tumbled sky… At such moments I am released from dependence on the future and to have no longings to be other than where I am.

JOHN LANE 1930 – 2012

Do we ever question the need to brush our teeth? Or say, "today I do not have time for brushing teeth?" Can we go a week without brushing? What would that be like? Please imagine it right now. How will the mouth and teeth feel? Do we believe if we brush teeth we will never need a dentist? And how about putting in a comparable amount of time, energy and regular practice to keep the mind clear, fresh, and refreshed? Or regularly brushing and clearing the mind from harmful residue? I view Mindfulness as a way of maintaining mental hygiene the same way brushing is needed for dental hygiene.

REZVAN AMELI

Mindfulness is being alive fully in the now.
Not wishing to change it and clouding it with
our anxieties, our phobias, our obsessions and
our stresses.

HAROLD DALTON

Happiness happens only in the present moment.
If you are happy now, there is nothing else to
accomplish. Indeed, if you become concerned
about whether you will be happy tomorrow or
even five minutes from now, you will forget to
be happy now. All your scheming and dreaming
takes you away from your present happiness.

PAUL FERRINI

You can't earn,
save or own happiness.
You can't buy it,
trade it or sell it.
It is an attitude.
An attitude of living.
An appreciation of life,
of love.
It can come to you.
Just be yourself, be mindful.
Just be.
Accept grace, accept love,
accept life.
It'll come to you.
Try it. You'll see.

DALTON EXLEY

Do we need to make a special effort to enjoy the beauty of the blue sky? Do we have to practice to be able to enjoy it? No, we just enjoy it. Each second, each minute of our lives can be like this. Wherever we are, any time, we have the capacity to enjoy the sunshine, the presence of each other, even the sensation of our breathing. We don't need to go to China to enjoy the blue sky. We don't have to travel into the future to enjoy our breathing. We can be in touch with these things right now.

THICH NHAT HANH, B. 1926

Deep in the soul, below pain, below all the distraction of life, is a silence vast and grand – an infinite ocean of calm, which nothing can disturb; nature's own exceeding peace, which "passes understanding". That which we seek with passionate longing, here and there, upward and outward; we find at last within ourselves.

C.M.C., B. 1844

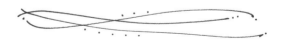

I will breathe.
I will think of solutions.
I will not let my worry control me.
I will not let me stress break me.
I will simply breathe.
And it will be okay...

SHAYNE MCCLENDON

None of us is promised tomorrow. Today,
in all its beauty and sadness and complexity,
is all we have. This light we see may be the last
such day we have on this earth. There is no
certainty, beyond the fact that one day we will
have no tomorrow, and that it is not ours to
know when that day will be.

KENT NERBURN, B. 1946

The whispers of rustling pine boughs. Flowers blooming. The beautiful blue sky. Fluffy white clouds. The smile of a neighbour. Each of these is a small miracle of life that has the capacity to nourish and heal us. They're there for us right now. The question is: are we there for them? If we're constantly running around, if our mind is caught up in endless planning and worrying, it's as if all these wonders don't even exist.

THICH NHAT HANH, B. 1926

I lay in a meadow until the unwrinkled serenity entered into my bones, and made me into one with the browsing kine, the still greenery, the drifting clouds, and the swooping birds.

ALICE JAMES 1848 – 1892

If *the doors of perception were cleansed everything would appear to us as it is, infinite.*

WILLIAM BLAKE 1757 – 1827

Take time to dream —
It is hitching your wagon to a star.
Take time to love and to be loved —
Take time to look around —
It is too short a day to be closed in.
Take time to laugh —
It is the music of the soul.

FROM AN OLD ENGLISH SAMPLER

If we had keen vision of all that is ordinary in human life, it would be like hearing the grass grow or the squirrel's heartbeat, and we should die of that roar which is the other side of silence.

GEORGE ELIOT (MARY ANN EVANS) 1819 – 1880

THE BASIC MINDFUL EXERCISE…

The basic mindful exercise
is to breathe in and breathe out.
Do it often. And sometimes do it
an extra time –
perhaps where and when you've
never done it before.
If any thoughts arise notice them,
but don't be judgemental or try
and change anything,
or "do" anything. Just notice,
just be aware.
Notice any tensions,
tightness or other sensations in your body.
Sense the world around you.

DALTON EXLEY

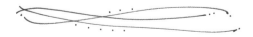

It is eternity now. I am in the midst of it. It is about me in the sunshine; I am in it, as the butterfly floats in the light-laden air. Nothing has to come; it is now. Now is eternity.

RICHARD JEFFERIES 1848 – 1887

Do not say, "It is morning," and dismiss it with a name of yesterday. See it for the first time as a new-born child that has no name.

RABINDRANATH TAGORE 1861 – 1941

Yesterday has gone.
Tomorrow may never come.
There is only the miracle
of this moment.
Savour it.
It is a gift.

MARIE STILKIND

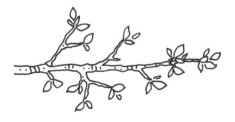

To be content
with what we possess
is the greatest
and most secure
of riches.

MARCUS TULLIUS CICERO 106 B.C. – 43 B.C.

You can throw yourself flat on the ground, stretched out upon Mother Earth, with the certain conviction that you are one with her and she with you. You are as firmly established, as invulnerable as she, indeed a thousand times firmer and more invulnerable. As surely as she will engulf you tomorrow, so surely will she bring you forth anew to new striving and suffering. And not merely "someday:" now, today, every day she is bringing you forth, not once but thousands of times, just as every day she engulfs you a thousand times over. For eternally and always there is only now, one and the same now; the present is the only thing that has no end.

ERWIN SCHRODINGER 1887 - 1961

I am going to venture that the man who sat on the ground in his tipi meditating on life and its meaning, accepting the kinship of all creatures, and acknowledging unity with the universe of things was infusing into his being the true essence of civilisation. And when native man left off this form of development, his humanization was retarded in growth.

LUTHER STANDING BEAR
(OGLALA SIOUX CHIEF) 1868 – 1939

The quieter you becom

To see a World in a Grain of Sand,
And a Heaven in a Wild Flower,
Hold infinity in the palm of your hand
and Eternity in an hour.

WILLIAM BLAKE 1757 – 1827

ie more you can hear.

BABA RAM DASS, B. 1931

At a certain point you say to the woods, to
the sea, to the mountains, to the world.
Now I am ready. Now I will stop and be wholly
attentive. You empty yourself and wait, listening.
After a time you hear it: there is nothing there.
There is nothing but those things only, those
created objects, discrete, growing or holding,
or swaying, or being rained on or raining, held,
flooding, or ebbing, standing, or spread. You feel
the world's word as a tension, a hum, a single
chorused note everywhere the same. This is it:
this hum is the silence...

ANNIE DILLARD, B. 1945

The siler

I'm filled with joy
when the day dawns
quietly
over the roof of the sky.

ESKIMO LOVE SONG

Quieten your mind and close your eyes.

Be still.

Feel the sun upon your face.

Hear the shrill of bird song.

Rejoice in your senses.

Rejoice in life.

PAM BROWN 1928 – 2014

Think of all this fleeting world:
A star at dawn, a bubble in a stream;
A flash of lightning in a summer cloud,
A flickering lamp, a phantom and a dream.

GAUTAMA BUDDHA c.563 B.C. – 483 B.C.

Try to be mindful, and let things take their natural course. Then your mind will become still in any surroundings, like a clear forest pool. All kinds of wonderful, rare animals will come to drink at the pool, and you will clearly see the nature of all things.

ACHAAN CHAH

Meditation
can help us embrace
our worries,
our fear,
our anger;
and that is very healing.
We let our own
natural capacity
for healing
do the work.

THICH NHAT HANH, B. 1926

In meditation,
we breathe
in the golden light
of health and wholeness
and breathe out
the darkness of pain
and suffering and hatred.

SUZANNE C. COLE

Life is fragile, like the dew hanging delicately on the grass, crystal drops that will be carried away on the first morning breeze.

DILGO KHYENTSE RINPOCHE 1910 – 1991

When compassion fills my heart,
free from all desire,
I sit quietly like the earth.
My silent cry echoes like thunder
throughout the universe.

JALAL AL-DIN MUHAMMAD RUMI 1207 – 1273

Look at everything as though you were seeing it either for the first or last time. Then your time will be filled with glory.

BETTY SMITH

An inch of time
is an inch of gold:
Treasure it.
Appreciate its fleeting nature;
Misplaced gold
is easily found,
misspent time
is lost forever.

LOY CHING-YUEN

Everything in the end passes. Everything in your life in the end passes. Celebrate your existence while you have it! Every day. All that you love, all that you live for, these are the things that matter. Yes, be mindful. Yes, of course be mindful and live your life to the full.

DALTON EXLEY

The beauty of the trees, the softness of the air, the fragrance of the grass, speak to me…
The faintness of the stars, the freshness of the morning, the dewdrop on the flower, speak to me… And my heart soars.

CHIEF DAN GEORGE, COAST SALISH 1899 – 1981

One cannot appreciate beauty on the run. When I can be motionless long enough, there is no limit I have ever reached to the revelations in an opening bud.

VIDA D. SCUDDER 1861 – 1954

Walk as if you are kissin

e Earth with your feet.

THICH NHAT HANH, B. 1926

Each moment is absolute, alive, and significant.
The frog leaps, the cricket sings, a dewdrop
glitters on the lotus leaf, a breeze passes through
the pine branches and the moonlight falls on the
murmuring stream.

D.T. SUZUKI

There's joy all around us!
Why wait till tomorrow?
We've only this moment to live.
A heaven within us
Is ours for the finding,
A freedom no riches can give!

J. DONALD WALTERS 1926 – 2013

A shaft of sunlight at the end of a dark
afternoon, a note in music, and the way the back
of a baby's neck smells...
Those are the important things.

E. B. WHITE 1899 – 1985

Normal day, let me be aware of the treasure you are. Let me not pass you by in quest of some rare and perfect tomorrow.

MARY JEAN IRION

Sit down,
wherever you are
and listen to the wind
that is singing
in your veins.

JOHN WELWOOD, B. 1943

Don't be so good at preparing for the future, at planning, planning, planning, that you forget to live today. In all this planning, planning for promotion, or to get a better car, or a bigger house, or greater wealth – everything is for tomorrow. All those todays sacrificed for tomorrows.

DALTON EXLEY

In order to swim one takes off all one's clothes – in order to aspire to the truth one must undress in a far more inward sense, divest oneself of all one's inward clothes, of thoughts, conceptions, selfishness, etc., before one is sufficiently naked.

SØREN KIERKEGAARD 1813 – 1855

Don't over-complicate mindfulness and make work out of it. We don't need to practice to enjoy the sunrise over mountains, or the sunset on a beach. What do we need to learn about the beauty of flowers and the deep blue of the sky?

D. E. HAROLD

Perhaps this very instant is your time... your own, your peculiar, your promised and presaged moment, out of all moments forever.

LOUISE BOGAN 1897 – 1970

REMEMBER TO PRACTISE
MINDFULNESS EXERCISES
Simply sit comfortably
and well-supported in a chair.
Close your eyes and become aware
of where your body is –
your feet on the floor,
the backs of your legs against the chair,
your thighs, buttocks, and back.
Notice any sounds or smells.
Breathe in and out.

DALTON EXLEY

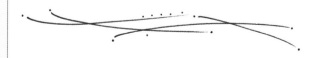

You don't need the iPhone: you have the most exquisite apparatus in the known universe sitting right in your head – the most complex organization of matter in the entire universe. And here are we, feeling a little depressed, feeling like we're not getting where we need to be, when really you might be exactly where you need to be.

JON KABAT-ZINN, B. 1944

The faculty of voluntarily bringing back a wandering attention over and over again, is the very root of judgement, character and will. An education which should improve this faculty would be the education par excellence.

WILLIAM JAMES 1842 – 1910

Surely there is something in the unruffled calm of nature that overawes our little anxieties and doubt: the sight of the deep blue sky and the clustering stars above, seem to impart a quiet to the mind.

JONATHAN EDWARDS

The thing which we speak of as beauty
does not have to be sought in distant lands...
It is here about us or it is nowhere...

ALLEN TUCKER

The air is full of sounds,
sighs of the wind in the trees,
sighs which fade back
into the overhanging silence.
A bee passes,
a golden ripple in the quiet air.

MARION MILNER 1900 – 1998

If you consider all the people
you know who seem truly happy,
there is likely to be one trait —
one essential perspective
on life — that each of these
happy people share...
It is the word now.
It is the understanding
that happiness exists
at just one time.
And that time is now.

WILLIE NELSON, B. 1933

Now

Without stirring abroad one can know the
whole world;
Without looking out of the window one can see
the way of heaven.
– The further one goes the less one knows.

LAO TZU 604 B.C. – 531 B.C.

Mindfulness helps you go home to the present.
And every time you go there and recognize a
condition of happiness that you have,
happiness comes.

THICH NHAT HANH, B. 1926

...this was the simple happiness of complete
harmony with her surroundings, the happiness
that asks for nothing, that just accepts,
just breathes, just is.

COUNTESS ELIZABETH VON ARNIM 1866 – 1941

Listen in deep silence.
Be very still and open your mind...
Sink deep into the peace
that waits for you beyond the frantic,
riotous thoughts
and sights and sounds of
this insane world.

FROM "A COURSE IN MIRACLES"

The fall of a leaf is

What is Life? It is the flash of a firefly in the night.
It is the breath of a buffalo in the winter time. It is
the little shadow which runs across the grass and
loses itself in the sunset.

CROWFOOT, BLACKFOOT INDIAN LEADER

Let us fill our hearts
with our own compassion –
towards ourselves
and towards all living beings.

THICH NHAT HANH, B. 1926

vhisper to the living.

RUSSIAN PROVERB

You don't have to like it – you just have to do it!
By the time you have been practicing every day
for eight weeks, you will have enough momentum
and direct personal experience with the practice
to keep going with it – for years or for life if you
choose to.

JON KABAT-ZINN, B. 1944

...I know nothing else but miracles...
To me every hour of the light
and dark is a miracle,
Every cubic inch of space is a miracle,
Every square yard of the surface
of the earth is spread with the same,
Every foot of the interior swarms with the same.

WALT WHITMAN 1819 – 1892

CLOSE TO THE EARTH

Come to a quiet place,
A place so quiet
That you can hear
The grass grow.
Lie on the soft grass,
Run your fingers
Through the softness
Of its petals,
And listen:
Listen to the earth.
The warm earth,
The life pulse
Of us all.

ALICE TAYLOR

The usefulness of a pot com

I love to spend time in nature, the wilder the better. Still water, grass blown gently by the wind, silence. Here with this precious time, the sun and the stars, the wild enters. The wild... that isn't taxed with grief or stress. Just this bright day. For a brief while I am free in the grace of this world.

DALTON EXLEY

Simply be. Be aware of what is happening right now. Stop dreaming about how your life might be different. Don't continually deny the present. Enjoy the now. Enjoy each day.

D. E. HAROLD

om its emptiness.

LAO TZU 604 B.C. – 531 B.C.

Many emotional disorders are characterized by a mind that gets high-jacked – usually from thoughts that they are trying to address or repair. Meditation allows an individual to simply watch the mind and still the mind allowing it to do what it does...

DR. ZINDEL SEGAL, B. 1956

Earth teach me
stillness as the grasses are stilled
with light.
Earth teach me
humility as blossoms are humble
with beginning.
Earth teach me
courage as the tree which stands
all alone.
Earth teach me
limitation as the ant which crawls
on the ground.

Earth teach me
freedom as the eagle which soars
in the sky.
Earth teach me
resignation as the leaves
which die in the autumn.
Earth teach me
regeneration as the seed
which rises in the spring.
Earth teach me
to forget myself as melted snow
forgets its life.

UTE PRAYER

A MINDFULNESS OF
PHYSICAL DISCOMFORT EXERCISE
Focus your attention on breathing.
Just observe.
Then shift attention to your body –
which areas are comfortable,
which uncomfortable?
See if you can feel those different sensations.
If thoughts pop into your head, observe,
but don't act on them.
Notice how sensations shift,
or diminish your attention
to other areas of discomfort.
To close, bring your attention
back to your breathing.
Many people are astonished
that by simply being aware of discomforts,
they lessen. Try it.

DALTON EXLEY

Granted, an hour of sensory tuning-in at the beach, by the stream, under the shade tree, on the nature trail, or atop the wind-swept butte won't fix all the broken stuff in our lives, but it will pull us out of our writhing minds, and into our grounded, flowing senses.

PHILIP S. CHARD

Between the in-breath and the out-breath lies the possibility of the future.

RESHAD FEILD, B. 1934

Those in a hurr

Peace means
loyalty to self...
And loyalty to one's self
means never a gap
between thought,
speech, act.

RUTH BEEBE HILL 1913 – 2015

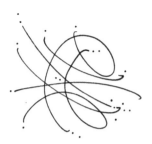

o not arrive. ZEN WISDOM

In Asian languages, the word for "mind" and the word for "heart" are the same. So if you're not hearing mindfulness in some deep way as heartfulness, you're not really understanding it. Compassion and kindness towards oneself are intrinsically woven into it. You could think of mindfulness as wise and affectionate attention.

JON KABAT-ZINN, B. 1944

Try looking at your mind
as a wayward puppy
that you are trying to paper train.
You don't drop-kick
a puppy into the neighbor's yard every
time it piddles
on the floor.
You just keep bringing it back
to the newspaper.

ANNE LAMOTT, B. 1954

You must live in the present, launch yourself on every wave, find your eternity in each moment. Fools stand on their island of opportunities and look toward another land. There is no other land; there is no other life but this.

HENRY DAVID THOREAU 1817 – 1862

Just slow down. Slow down your speech. Slow down your breathing. Slow down your walking. Slow down your eating. And let this slower, steadier pace perfume your mind. Just slow down...

DOKO

The dream was always
running ahead of one.
To catch up,
to live for a moment
in unison with it,
that was the miracle.

ANAÏS NIN 1903 – 1977

The sunlight dapples
through the trees, the apple falls.
Be quiet. Be at peace.

HELEN EXLEY

Even in these rushed days
there is such peace between.
There are moments
when two eagle feathers can fill me
with joy; when the last rays
of the sun touch my forehead
as I stand by the kitchen door...
when even the wind is part
of it all. Surely such moments
do something to me.
If not, it is because
I hide beneath the pettiness.

EDITH WARNER 1892 – 1951

There are two days in the week about which and upon which I never worry. Two carefree days, kept sacredly free from fear and apprehension. One of the days is Yesterday.... And the other day I do not worry about is Tomorrow.

ROBERT JONES BURDETTE 1844 – 1914

If you concentrate on finding whatever is good in every situation, you will discover that your life will suddenly be filled with gratitude, a feeling that nurtures the soul.

RABBI HAROLD KUSHNER

...I keep trying gently to bring my mind back to what is really there to be seen, maybe to be seen and noted with a kind of reverence.

ANNE LAMOTT, B. 1954

There are only two ways
to live your life.
One is as though
nothing is a miracle.
The other is as though
everything is a miracle.

ALBERT EINSTEIN 1879 – 1955

Miracle

I was set free! I dissolved in the sea, because white sails and flying spray, became beauty and rhythm, became moonlight and the ship and the high dim-starred sky! I belonged, without past or future, within peace and unity and a wild joy, within something greater than my own life, or the life of Man, to Life itself!

EUGENE O'NEILL 1888 – 1953

The whole of life is but a point of time, let us enjoy it, therefore, while it lasts.

PLUTARCH A.D. 46 – A.D. 120

If we are not in this present millisecond of life and conscious experience, we are not alive; we are merely thinking our lives. Yet we have seen so many die, looking back over their shoulders at their lives, shaking their heads and muttering in bewilderment, "What was that all about?"

STEPHEN LEVINE, B. 1937

Oh, this is the joy of the ros

Over all the mountaintops is peace. In all treetops you perceive scarcely a breath. The little birds in the forest are silent. Wait then; soon you, too, will have peace.

JOHANN WOLFGANG VON GOETHE 1749 – 1832

The lure of the distant
and the difficult is deceptive.
The great opportunity
is where you are.

JOHN BURROUGHS 1837 – 1921

at it blows, and goes.

WILLA CATHER 1873 – 1947

In meditation we discover our inherent restlessness. Sometimes we get up and leave. Sometimes we sit there but our bodies wiggle and squirm and our minds go far away. This can be so uncomfortable that we feel it's impossible to stay. Yet this feeling can teach us not just about ourselves but what it is to be human... It goes against the grain to stay present. These are the times when only gentleness and a sense of humour can give us the strength to settle down... So whenever we wander off, we gently encourage ourselves to "stay" and settle down. Are we experiencing restlessness? Stay! Are fear and loathing out of control? Stay! Aching knees and throbbing back? Stay! What's for lunch? Stay! I can't stand this another minute! Stay!

PEMA CHODRON, B. 1936

The real
meditation
practice
is how we live
our lives
from moment
to moment
to moment.

JON KABAT-ZINN, B. 1944

THE MINDFUL IMMERSION EXERCISE

This exercise is about escaping
from the constant stress and strivings
of our daily routines and cultivating
an appreciation, a contentment in being.
It's a challenge to choose a regular chore
you don't particularly like;
clearing up or doing the hoovering.
Instead of rushing the job,
try relaxing into it, taking your time
and immersing yourself in it.
You might surprise yourself
by actually enjoying clearing up,
you never know!

DALTON EXLEY

Among the mind's powers is one that comes
of itself to many children and artists.
It need not be lost, to the end of our days,
by anyone who has ever had it.
This is the power of taking delight in a thing,
or rather in anything, not as a means
to some other end, but just because it is
what it is. A child in the full health
of his mind will put his hand flat
on the summer turf, feel it,
and give a little shiver of private glee
at the elastic firmness of the globe.

CHARLES EDWARD MONTAGUE 1867 – 1928

Be here

True self is non-self, the awareness that the self is made only of non-self elements.
There's no separation between self and other, and everything is interconnected.
Once you are aware of that you are no longer caught in the idea that you are a separate entity.

THICH NHAT HANH, B. 1926

Death and transformation are our unchosen and unchangeable fate. All that we can choose and change is consciousness. But to change this is to change all.

RODNEY COLLIN

now. BABA RAM DASS, B. 1931

In the midst of movement and chaos, keep stillness inside of you.

DEEPAK CHOPRA, B. 1947

Lie gently in the dark
and listen to the rain pattering against the glass,
the swish of passing cars,
the hush of leaves.
Renounce decisions, speculation,
the tug of time.
The world beyond the window
enfolds your silence, holds you softly. Sleep.

PAM BROWN 1928 – 2014

...Listen to

Gradually, a few moments one day, more moments the next, being there in that small safe woodland began to seem almost the same experience as making music, as the way, when I played the piano, I was the music... I had no consciousness of my individual self.

SALLY CARRIGHAR 1905 – 1986

As you simplify your life,
the laws of the universe will be simpler;
solitude will not be solitude,
poverty will not be poverty,
nor weakness weakness.

HENRY DAVID THOREAU 1817 – 1862

Forever is compose

We are the Earth, through the plants and
animals that nourish us. We are the rains and
the oceans that flow through our veins. We are
the breath of the forests of the land, and the
plants of the sea... Linked in a web of
community, we are all interconnected.

D.T. SUZUKI

f nows. EMILY DICKINSON 1830 – 1886

Why is it that I find it so hard to take time for myself? Time to be, rather than time to do. And often what is urgent elbows its way to the forefront of my day and the important gets trampled in the rush.

MARION STROUD

Here are the veins of your hand and here are the veins of a leaf. Here branches stretch out against the sky. Here streams run to meet the river. We are bound together. The same life flows through all things. Be happy in this unity, this continuity.

PAM BROWN 1928 – 2014

There is beauty around us, in things large and small, in friends, family, the countryside, a singing bird. Stop to reflect, to give thanks, to contemplate the gift of another day. Touch the wonders of life and rejoice.

ANTON CHEKHOV 1860 – 1904

Our original nature is,
in the highest truth,
void, silent, pure;
it is glorious and mysterious
peaceful joy — and that is all.
Enter deeply into it
by awakening to it yourself.
That which is before you
is it, in all its fullness,
utterly complete.

HUANG PO

A MINDFULNESS EATING EXERCISE

Choose some food you like,
maybe a piece of fruit or chocolate.
Imagine you've never seen it before,
explore it with your eyes, feel its texture,
its shape. Smell it. Place it in your mouth,
but don't bite yet. Roll it around your tongue,
note the sensations. Slowly chew,
tasting it fully. Don't swallow yet,
allow yourself to savour it.
Finally,
be aware of the feeling of swallowing.
This is mindful eating.

DALTON EXLEY

To my mind anyone who turns away from nature, whose head is forever filled with thoughts of keeping up this and keeping up that...
Oh, going on like that, one so easily arrives at a point where one can no longer tell white from black.

VINCENT VAN GOGH 1853 – 1890

When you look at the sun during your walking meditation, the mindfulness of the body helps you to see that the sun is in you; without the sun there is no life at all and suddenly you get in touch with the sun in a different way.

THICH NHAT HANH, B. 1926

If you truly get in touch with a piece of carrot, you get in touch with the soil, the rain, the sunshine. You get in touch with Mother Earth and eating in such a way, you feel in touch with true life, your roots, and that is meditation.
If we chew every morsel of our food in that way we become grateful and when you are grateful, you are happy.

THICH NHAT HANH, B. 1926

It is good to be alone in a garden at dawn or dark so that all its shy presences may haunt you and possess you in a reverie of suspended thought.

JAMES DOUGLAS

To drop into being means to recognize your interconnectedness with all life, and with being itself. Your very nature is being part of larger and larger spheres of wholeness.

JON KABAT-ZINN, B. 1944

Whatever the present moment contains, accept it as if you had chosen it. Always work with it, not against it.

ECKHART TOLLE, B. 1948

Be *happy*
in the moment,
that's enough.
Each *moment*
is all we need,
not more.

MOTHER TERESA 1910 – 1997

"If it were just a matter of playing football with the firmament, stirring up the ocean, turning back rivers, carrying away mountains, I could manage it easily enough" said Monkey. "But if it comes to sitting still and meditating, I am bound to come off badly. It's quite against my nature to sit still."

WU CHENG'EN 1500 – 1582

That it will never
come again
is what makes life
so sweet.

EMILY DICKINSON 1830 – 1886

It is possible to lose money, wealth, position, status, friends, even love and win these back. Time is the one thing you can never win back. Spend each moment wisely. Enjoy your time. You will never get it back again.

DALTON EXLEY

Time

Grant yourself a moment of peace and you will understand how foolishly you have scurried about. Learn to be silent and you will notice that you have talked too much.
Be kind and you will realise that your judgement of others was too severe.

TSCHEN TSCHI JU

You should let go and make yourself empty and quiet, clear and calm.

YING AN

Where there is peace and meditation, there is neither anxiety nor doubt.

ST. FRANCIS OF ASSISI 1181 – 1226

The ultimate value of life depends upon awareness and the power of contemplation rather than upon mere survival.

ARISTOTLE 384 B.C. – 322 B.C.

One of the conclusions I have come to in my old age is the importance of living in the ever-present now. In the past, too often I indulged in the belief that somehow or other tomorrow would be brighter or happier or richer.

RUTH CASEY

This isn't just
"another day, another dollar."
It's more like
"another day,
another miracle."

VICTORIA MORAN

It's the scent of the roses that fills the air,
And the whispering wind blowing through
my hair.
It's the sparkling dew drops on the ground,
And the gurgling stream that makes hardly
a sound.
It's the feel of the snowflakes that melt on my
tongue.
And the night owl calling to her young.

ELIZABETH ANNE DE GREY

Lost yesterday
somewhere between sunrise and sunset
two golden hours
each set with sixty diamond minutes.
No reward is offered for they are gone forever.

HORACE MANN 1796 – 1859

Spend all you have for loveliness,
Buy it and never count the cost;
For one white singing hour of peace.
Count many a year of strife well lost,
And for a breath of ecstasy
Give all that you have been, or could be.

SARA TEASDALE 1884 – 1933

EXERCISE: JUST BEING IN THE NOW

Sit or lie down and direct your attention
to the present moment.
Calm your mind, remind yourself
that all things pass.
Sense your body, ask yourself if
there is anywhere you can let go of tension,
and release it.
Let thoughts come into your mind,
but just note them and any associated
feelings – positive or negative –
just observe them, observe yourself.
Be aware of your body,
your breath, your mind,
your emotions.
Accept this moment in time.

DALTON EXLEY

If something is lacking
in your perspective –
if something is missing in your heart –
then despite the most luxurious
surroundings, you cannot be happy.
However, if you have peace of mind,
you can find happiness
even under the most difficult
circumstances.

THE DALAI LAMA, B. 1935

Suddenly the heart lifts with joy
– finding itself part of all that is.
Sunlight and cloud,
trees, rivers,
wild geese flying.
A moment's glory.

CHARLOTTE GRAY

Do not dwell in the past,
do not dream of the future,
concentrate the mind
on the present moment.

GAUTAMA BUDDHA c.563 B.C. – 483 B.C.

Ten thousand flowers in spring,
the moon in autumn,
a cool breeze in summer,
snow in winter.
If your mind isn't clouded by
unnecessary things,
this is the best season of your life.

WU-MEN 1183 – 1260

Each day provide

Be tough in the way a blade of grass is: rooted, willing to lean, and at peace with what is around it.

NATALIE GOLDBERG

Each day has a rarity... I could put it in a vase and admire it, like the first dandelions...

MARGARET LAWRENCE 1896 – 1973

ts own gifts.

MARTIAL c.40 – c.104

Each time for the first time.
Each moment the only moment.

JON KABAT-ZINN, B. 1944

May the wind be gentle
May the waves be calm
May the elements
smile on all our wishes.

WOLFGANG AMADEUS MOZART 1756 - 1791

There is in all things an inexhaustible
sweetness and purity, a silence that is a
fountain of action and joy. It rises up in
wordless gentleness and flows out to me
from unseen roots of all created being.

THOMAS MERTON 1915 – 1968

Joyously,
drunkenly,
serenely,
divinely
aware.

HENRY MILLER 1891 – 1980

The moment one gives
close attention to anything,
even a blade of grass,
it becomes a mysterious,
awesome,
indescribably
magnificent world
in itself.

HENRY MILLER 1891 – 1980

If my heart can become pure
and simple like
that of a child,
I think there probably
can be no greater happiness
than this.

KITARO NISHIDA

*Nobody sees
a flower really;
it is so small.
We haven't time,
and to see
takes time.*

GEORGIA O'KEEFE 1887 – 1986

A STANDING MINDFULNESS EXERCISE

Stand still for a while,
noticing how your body connects
to the ground.
Become aware of your surroundings,
the sights, sounds and smells.
Notice, but don't try to change
your breath as it moves in and out.
You can do this whenever you want
during the day.

DALTON EXLEY

The soil was soothing, strengthening, cleansing and healing. That is why the old Indian still sits upon the earth instead of propping himself up away from its life-giving forces. For him, to sit or lie upon the ground is to be able to think more deeply and feel more keenly.

LUTHER STANDING BEAR (OGLALA SIOUX CHIEF) 1868 – 1939

Reality is a flowing. This does not mean that everything moves, changes, becomes. Science and common experience tell us that. It means that movement, change, becoming is everything that there is. There is nothing else; everything is movement, is change. The time that we ordinarily think about is not real time, but a picture of space.

HENRI-LOUIS BERGSON 1859 – 1941

Sitting quietly,

doing nothing,

Spring comes

and the grass

grows by itself.

BASHO 1644 – 1694

Look to this day! Look to this day! For it is life, the very life of life. In its brief course lie all the varieties and realities of your existence: the bliss of growth, the glory of action, the splendour of beauty. For yesterday is already a dream and tomorrow is only a vision but today, well-lived, makes every yesterday a dream of happiness, and every tomorrow a vision of hope. Look well, therefore, to this day! Such is the salutation of the dawn.

SANSKRIT

You ask why I make my home in the mountain forest, and I smile, and am silent, and even my soul remains quiet: it lives in the other world which no one owns. The peach trees blossom. The water flows.

LI PO 701 – 762

Each second you can be reborn. Each second there can be a new beginning. It is choice, it is your choice.

CLEARWATER

After a lovely day out of doors by myself I saw that a single act of admiration is of little use. We must live with beauty, without any straining effort to admire, quietly attentive, absorbent, until by degrees the beauty becomes one with us and alters our blood.

MARK RUTHERFORD 1831 – 1913

My life has no purpose, no direction, no aim, no meaning and yet I'm happy. I can't figure it out. What am I doing right?

CHARLES M. SCHULZ 1922 – 2000

The mind
is never right
but when it is at peace
within itself.

SENECA THE YOUNGER 4 B.C. – A.D. 65

PEACE

The secret of seeing things
as they are is to take off our
coloured spectacles.
That being-as-it-is,
with nothing extraordinary
about it, nothing wonderful,
is the great wonder.

MASTER SESSAN

*The person
is richest
who is content
with the least.*

SOCRATES 469 B.C. – 399 B.C.

Solitude, quality solitude, is an assertion of self-worth, because only in the stillness can we hear the truth of our own unique voices.

PEARL CLEAGE

He is happiest, be he king or peasant, who finds peace in his home.

JOHANN WOLFGANG VON GOETHE 1749 – 1832

Try dying every day to your old self... So that you emerge renewed and young again as the tired mind sheds its load...

KRISTIN ZAMBUCKA

A happy life is not built up of tours abroad and pleasant holidays, but of little clumps of violets noticed by the roadside.

DR. EDWARD A. WILSON

When anxiety hovers above your light and shadows and all your actions, please do not fear them too much. I would like to remind you that life has not forgotten you. It is holding you by your hand and will not let you fall.

Why do you want to shut out of your life any uneasiness or any depression? For after all, even though you do not know now where all of this will lead, these experiences may lead to the change that you were always hoping for.

RAINER MARIA RILKE 1875 – 1926

Never be in a hurry; do everything quietly and in a calm spirit. Do not lose your inner peace for anything whatsoever, even if your whole world seems upset.

SAINT FRANCIS DE SALES 1567 – 1622

BEING NON-JUDGEMENTAL
ABOUT FEELINGS

Feelings are often labelled good
or positive (confident, brave, upbeat)
or negative (fearful, angry, sad, depressive).
In mindfulness, feelings are not judged
as good or bad, they just are what they are.
We tend to find some emotions difficult,
or uncomfortable, and others easier.
Rather than feeling that we mustn't feel sad
or scared or down, in mindfulness
we simply observe these feelings
and emotions with curiosity,
non-judgementally accepting them.

DALTON EXLEY

Don't hurry,
don't worry.
You're only here
for a short visit.
So be sure
to stop and smell
the flowers.

WALTER HAGEN 1892 – 1969

Don't mortgage today for the promise of a better life tomorrow. Plan for the future? Yes, yes, of course, but live today, live each day.

D. E. HAROLD

To the mind that is still, the whole universe surrenders.

LAO TZU 604 B.C. – 531 B.C.

Happiness cannot be travelled to, owned, earned, worn or consumed. Happiness is the spiritual experience of living every minute with love, grace, and gratitude.

DENIS WAITLEY, B. 1933

Our true home
is in the present moment.
To live in the present moment
is a miracle.
The miracle is not to walk on water.
The miracle is to walk
on the green Earth
in the present moment,
to appreciate the peace
and beauty that are available now.

THICH NHAT HANH, B. 1926

Mindfulness
is like waking
from a long hibernation
and suddenly seeing
a world so beautiful
it takes your
breath away.

DALTON EXLEY

The silence
which vibrates around
contains more sense of
presence than sound.

CATHERINE HEWITT

Let us not therefore go hurrying about and collecting honey, bee-like, buzzing here and there impatiently from a knowledge of what is to be arrived at. But let us open out like leaves of a flower, and be passive and receptive: ... taking hints from every noble insect that favours us with a visit.

JOHN KEATS 1795 - 1821

A wise person does not value a large jade but cherishes a moment of time, for time is difficult to keep and very easy to lose.

CHINESE SAYING

A moment

Mindfulness helps us focus on one thing at a time. Be it this moment in time, or one goal you have. It helps you be patient, find peace, focus, find kindness, find creative awareness, whatever you choose, it is your mindfulness.

DALTON EXLEY

If every eight-year-old
in the world
is taught meditation,
we will eliminate violence
from the world
within one generation.

THE DALAI LAMA, B. 1935

The birds have vanished
down the sky.
Now the last cloud drains away.
We sit together,
the mountain and I,
until only the
mountain remains.

LI PO 701 – 762

Only in quietness
can the infinity of wonder
find you.

PAM BROWN 1928 – 2014

Between the stirrup and the ground
there is always hope.
Between stimulus and response
there is always space.
Therein lies our potential,
our freedom, our choice,
our growth.

DALTON EXLEY

Carpenters bend wood;
fletchers bend arrows;
wise people fashion themselves.

GAUTAMA BUDDHA c.563 B.C. – 483 B.C.

Every minute life begin

Nothing ever gets anywhere. The earth keeps turning round and gets nowhere. The moment is the only thing that counts.

JEAN COCTEAU 1889 – 1963

When I live in the now, I feel no real pain from the past. Imagined fear of the future can't harm me.

JOAN BURKA

ll over again.

THOMAS MERTON, 1915 – 1968

Those who are awake live in a state of constant amazement.

GAUTAMA BUDDHA c.563 B.C. – 483 B.C.

Beauty is all around us every day. In a million ways. When we release ourselves from endlessly planning and worrying, it is as if we can see again for the first time.

DALTON EXLEY

The morning sun,
the new sweet
earth and
the great silence.

T. C. MCLUHAN

The greatest
revelation
is stillness.

LAO TZU 604 B.C. – 531 B.C.

We tend to be alive in the future, not now.
We say, "Wait until I finish school and get my
PhD degree, and then I will be really alive."
When we have it, and it's not easy to get, we say
to ourselves, "I have to wait until I have a job in
order to be really alive." And then after the job,
a car. After the car, a house. We are not capable
of being alive in the present moment. We tend
to postpone being alive to the future, the distant
future, we don't know when. Now is the
moment to be alive. We may never be alive
at all in our entire life.

THICH NHAT HANH, B. 1926

Happiness,
not in another place
but this place...
not for another hour,
but this hour.

WALT WHITMAN 1819 – 1892

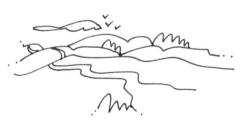

Paradise
is where I am.

VOLTAIRE 1694 – 1778

Time is but the stream I go a-fishing in.

HENRY DAVID THOREAU 1817 – 1862

All the suffering,
stress, and addiction
comes from not realizing
you already are
what you are looking for.

JON KABAT-ZINN, B. 1944

EXERCISE: BEING MINDFUL
OF YOUR THOUGHTS.
Start with being mindful of your breath.
Be quiet and still.
Notice any thoughts that pop up.
Don't judge or internalize these thoughts
as good or back, positive or negative.
If you notice you are struggling
with thinking about your thoughts,
notice this too as just another thought.
While you do this imagine your thoughts
floating by like clouds, or as words
written on water. Go with this
if it works for you.
Watch as thoughts come and go,
replaced by others.
Bring yourself back to your breath
to close this exercise.

DALTON EXLEY

We are always
getting ready to live,
but never living.

RALPH WALDO EMERSON 1803 – 1882

True joy

is serene.

SENECA THE YOUNGER 4 B.C. – A.D. 65

They had all lain still, thinking about this for a while. Somewhere, a long way off, a coyote called. "I guess that's all forever is," his father replied. "Just one long trail of nows. And I guess all you can do is try and live one now at a time without getting too worked up about the last now or the next now."

NICHOLAS EVANS, B. 1950

> *"Renew thyself*
> *completely each day;*
> *do it again,*
> *and again,*
> *and forever again."*

ON THE BATH TUB OF KING TCHING THANG
1748–1799

I am calmest when I am at my ranch. This is where I am able to forget about the pressures of being Pele, and I can for a time just be Edson. I rest. I relax. Thoughts about life, my obligations and the responsibilities I've gained, disappear. I like looking after the fish, the horses and even the pigs. I'm in touch with nature, and I enjoy the peace and quiet tremendously.

PELÉ, B. 1940

Einstein was right. You can live your life
as though nothing is a miracle
or as though everything is a miracle.
You can see magic in the tiniest atom
right out to the entire unfathomable
universe, or you can just see the particular
small world of your existence.
It is largely up to you how you perceive
the world.

DALTON EXLEY

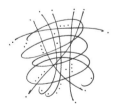

If we can just let go and trust
that things will work out
the way they're supposed to,
without trying to control
the outcome,
then we can begin to enjoy
the moment more fully.

GOLDIE HAWN, B. 1945

The best and sweetest things in life are things
you cannot buy: the music of the birds at dawn,
the rainbow in the sky. The dazzling magic
of the stars, the miracle of light.

PATIENCE STRONG 1907 – 1990

EXERCISE: LISTENING MINDFULLY
This exercise helps you broaden
your appreciation of sound.
It works best if you choose a piece of music
you don't know; you could listen
to the radio or put on headphones.
Close your eyes and really listen to the music.
Try not to judge it by genre or artist,
ignore these labels and just listen
to the sound.
Pick out different instruments;
give yourself permission
to let go of preconceptions
and get lost in the sound.

DALTON EXLEY

I am grateful for what I am and have. My thanksgiving is perpetual. It is surprising how contented one can be with nothing definite – only a sense of existence. My breath is sweet to me. O, how I laugh when I think of my vague indefinite riches. No run on my bank can drain it, for my wealth is not possession but enjoyment.

HENRY DAVID THOREAU 1817 – 1862

While washing the dishes one should only be washing the dishes, which means one should be completely aware of the fact that one is washing the dishes.

At first glance, that might seem a little silly. Why put so much stress on a simple thing? But that's precisely the point. The fact that I am standing there and washing these bowls is a wondrous reality. I am completely myself, following my breath, conscious of my presence, and conscious of my thoughts and actions.

There's no way I can be tossed around mindlessly like a bottle slapped here and there on the waves.

THICH NHAT HANH, B. 1926

If you want to

LEO TOLSTOY 1828 – 1910

Simplifying our lives does not mean sinking into idleness, but on the contrary, getting rid of the most subtle aspect of laziness: the one which makes us take on thousands of less important activities.

MATTHIEU RICARD, B. 1946

be happy, be.

Fear not for the future; weep not for the past.

PERCY BYSSHE SHELLEY 1792 – 1822

I expand
and live
in the warm day
like corn
and melons.

RALPH WALDO EMERSON 1803 – 1882

Happiness

Don't evaluate your life in terms of achievements, trivial or monumental, along the way... Instead, wake up and appreciate everything you encounter along the path. Enjoy the flowers that are there for your pleasure. Tune in to the sunrise, the little children, the laughter, the rain, and the birds. Drink it all in... there is no way to happiness; happiness is the way.

DR. WAYNE W. DYER, B. 1940

This is it.
No one else has the answer.
No other place will be better,
and it has already turned out.

At the centre of your being
you have the
answer;
you know who you are
and you know what you want.

LAO TZU 604 B.C. – 531 B.C.

Our life is frittered away with detail....
Simplify, simplify.

HENRY DAVID THOREAU 1817 – 1862

Living mindlessly takes an enormous toll.

ROGER WALSH

Outside noisy, inside empty.

CHINESE SAYING

Breathe out, look in, let go.

JOHN WELWOOD, B. 1943

You do not need
to leave your room...
Remain sitting at your table
and listen.
Do not even listen, simply wait.
Do not even wait,
be still and solitary.
The world will freely
offer itself to you
to be unmasked.
It has no choice.
It will roll in ecstasy
at your feet.

FRANZ KAFKA 1883 – 1924